ACHIEVE YOUR VISION

ALEX FREYTAG

ISBN: 978-0-9963-4441-8 (sc)
ISBN: 978-0-9963-4440-1 (e)

This book is also available in an e-book format,
available on many online platforms.

Because of the dynamic nature of the Internet, any web addresses or links contained in this book may have changed since publication and may no longer be valid. The views expressed in this work are solely those of the author and do not necessarily reflect the views of the publisher, and the publisher hereby disclaims any responsibility for them.

Any people depicted in stock imagery provided by Thinkstock are models, and such images are being used for illustrative purposes only. Certain stock imagery © Thinkstock.

Lulu Publishing Services rev. date: 1/5/2016

PRAISE FOR ACHIEVE YOUR VISION

A masterful collection of real life stories and practical tools that help business owners gain traction in their business.
  -Gino Wickman, Author of *Traction*, Founder, EOS® Worldwide

Achieve Your Vision is a crystal clear and profoundly useful book... a super-practical system for dropping the victim mentality and achieving real bottom-line results."
        -Steve Chandler, Best-selling author, motivational speaker

Alex Freytag and the ProfitWorks team work side-by-side with executives and business owners facing the challenges of turning vision into managed enterprises. *Achieve Your Vision* is the place to start for guidance in what to study, who to follow, and how to go.
        -Artie Isaac, Executive Coach, Speaker, Trainer

A clear, concise message that works in the real world. EOS® is working for our management team, our associates, and our stakeholders.
        -Ted Coons, Chairman & CEO, Spillman Company

A single source, offering impactful leadership tools and practices that any results-driven leader can immediately put into action.
        -Nataline Lomedico, CEO/President, Giroux Glass Inc.

A comprehensive summary and resource that sets the stage for Entrepreneurs to share their vision and lead their team to success!
        -Sandy L. King, President, Symbiont Service Corporation

This book is dedicated to my wife, Christine.

CONTENTS

INTRODUCTION

Many business owners feel challenged when trying to engage their employees in helping them achieve their vision. I decided to write this book to discuss these challenges, and share many ideas I have seen business owners use to address them. I have kept it short out of respect for your time as well as to recognize that other authors, many of whom I have referenced, have written in great detail on the 'how' already. I encourage you to read their works if you decide you'd like to read more about some of the concepts I discuss.

In addition to sharing some of my experiences, my ultimate goal is to inspire you to implement this methodology to get more control, gain more traction, achieve your vision, and ultimately build a better business and life for yourself. I want you to be in love with your business and hope you find this book to be valuable and inspiring. Let's get started with my discovery.

CHAPTER 1

My Discovery - The Leadership Team is Broken

I n early 1995, my father shared with my older brother and me a business idea he had. He'd been in business for many years and he felt that most employees have no idea how a company makes money or how much (or little) profit companies truly make. As a board member with the Central Ohio Center for Economic Education, he periodically interacted with university economics professors whose mission was to teach primary school teachers how to teach economics to kids.

A consummate entrepreneur, he thought that perhaps there was a business idea in teaching employees about economics, business and finance to help them begin to see the business from an owner's perspective. My brother and I thought this was a great idea, so we created a business plan and launched a company called ProfitWorks in 1996.

Although the initial idea was around training employees on economics and business, we quickly realized that in order for the lessons to have an impact, we'd have to include some real financial data from our client companies.

In recent years the fear of sharing financial information with employees has waned a bit, but initially we found there was a great deal of trepidation. Business owners asked us:

- What if I teach my employees about profit and then they leave?
- What if I don't teach them and they stay?
- What if they share the information with our competition?

- What's the purpose of sharing the information–they won't understand it anyway.
- Why should I care if my employees understand this stuff?

As you can imagine many business owners were not excited to share a lot of financial information with their employees, but we came to realize that enlightened business owners could see the value. Over the years, I have learned that the owners of the best companies put these fears aside; they realize that when their employees have good information, they make better decisions. They also realize the correlated positive effect: when they share more information with their employees, they build trust with their workforce, and the barrier between "us" and "them" lowers as open and honest communication increases.

The content of our original workshops began with the fundamental truth that profit is the engine of growth in a market economy. Without profit there is no incentive for anyone: owners, investors, management or employees. We developed content around this basic premise of profit motivation as a potential reward for risk taken. We included exercises to teach employees about risk, return and liquidity and the relationship between these concepts.

In the late 90s, I met Jack Stack who had published *The Great Game of Business* in 1994. I attended his annual gathering in Springfield, Missouri and learned a considerable amount about the path we saw great companies taking to engage their employees in transforming their businesses. I also met and worked with Brad Hams who had founded the company Ownership Thinking in 1995, and who published the book, *Ownership Thinking* in 2012. These visionaries, and others like them who had similar ideas about teaching employees about business, had the same basic goal of improving the financial performance of the company by helping their employees understand and focus on the measureables that they can affect. We all emphasized that financial literacy is *not* just about sharing financial information; it's about truly reaching the employees, inspiring them, and getting their hearts into business. It was a strong emphasis on culture.

Today we call this "healthy and smart." Most businesses are smart. They know how to deliver their product or service and make money. They are financially focused, and that's great. But most companies are not healthy. Healthy is the culture piece. Healthy is about solving business issues without blame and finger-pointing. It is about a united front and eliminating politics. It is about open and honest. And companies of excellence, truly great companies, are both healthy and smart.

Figure 1.1 Healthy and Smart

After a few years of working with companies to help them implement the business literacy and employee engagement system, I noticed a disturbing trend. From about 50% of the companies we taught, I was getting a call from the owner three to six months later saying, "Alex, your system isn't working!" We had designed scorecards and taught the leadership teams about measureables and the importance of having regular meetings, so I would naturally ask, "Tell me how your weekly meetings are going? Are you using the scorecard and forecasting against plan?" And the owner would inevitably say, "Well, we haven't started having our meetings yet." And as our conversation progressed, I would undoubtedly learn that the owner and his team were not using many, if any, of the employee engagement tools that we had developed together. My discovery was this: it wasn't that the system wasn't working; it was that the leadership team was broken!

I found that leadership team members were often rowing in different directions. They often weren't disciplined. They were overwhelmed by the day-to-day whirlwind. They didn't hold each other accountable. And in many cases they didn't believe that the employee engagement tools would work, so they didn't drive them.

And can you imagine asking your employees to follow you when you and your leadership team don't know or agree on where you're going?

CHAPTER 2

Credibility and Trust

I n so many cases, the leadership team of an organization is not on the same page. Or worse, they are so misaligned that their dysfunction completely sabotages any system's potential for success.

When your leadership team is completely aligned on where you are going and how you are going to get there, you have clarity. When your leadership team communicates that clarity to your entire company, you build credibility within the workforce. This idea of credibility is critical to establishing a potential for trust; in my experience, trust is the core of culture. It is the core of any relationship. Without trust you have no foundation upon which to build a thriving organization.

In *The 7 Habits of Highly Effective People*, Stephen R. Covey talks about a trust account that exists between two individuals. Each individual makes deposits into the metaphorical trust account that helps nurture the relationship and the relationship naturally grows. In the same way, individuals can make withdrawals from the trust account.

If you imagine a married couple, you can see how this metaphor plays out. The husband cooks dinner; he makes a deposit. The wife buys a pair of shoes for her husband that she thinks he might like; she makes a deposit. The husband forgets to tell his wife about an evening meeting and misses a planned family dinner; he makes a withdrawal. And so on. As long as there is a positive balance in the trust account, the relationship is in most cases not significantly damaged by these occasional withdrawals.

The same trust account can be said to exist between a

leadership team and the workforce. The trust account offers great potential for the company. And any company that is not building this account with the workforce is missing a huge opportunity. Figure 2.1 below identifies some of the Trust Builders and Trust Destroyers I commonly see in the workplace.

Trust Builders	Trust Destroyers
Transparency	Hidden agendas
Follow through	Say one thing and do another
Open and honest	Disrespect —Shooting down people/ideas
A handful of rules	Politics
Delegation	Micro-management
Fairness	Changing the rules in the middle of the game
A results-based workplace	A time-based workplace

Figure 2.1 Trust Builders and Trust Destroyers

What are the net effects of trust? In my experience, trust frees people. It provides autonomy. Dan Pink, author of *Drive*, says that autonomy is one of the three elements that truly motivates people (the others are mastery and purpose). Trust provides that autonomy. When people truly feel trusted they begin to take more risks, they learn and grow and they feel pride and a joy of accomplishment.

Also, when someone feels trusted they intrinsically have a sense of wholeness. They feel a part of a winning team with a common direction. They feel camaraderie with their team, respect, and a sense of belonging, which in Abraham Maslow's hierarchy is near the top (Figure 2.2).

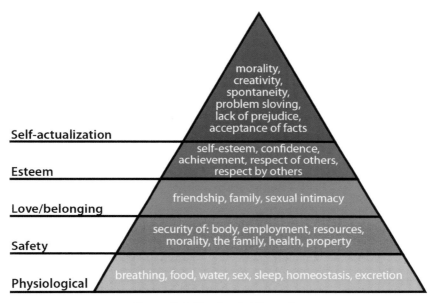

Figure 2.2 Maslow's Hierarchy

At the peak of Maslow's pyramid are growth needs, which are reflected in our innate desire to learn and grow once our deficiency needs (physiological, security, belonging, esteem) are met. The growth need and the drive toward self-actualization require special characteristics in an individual to reach their fullest potential.

A lack of trust in the workplace is a leadership issue. Gallup's 2013 survey indicated (yet again) that 70% of employees are not engaged in their company. In fact 20% are actively disengaged, meaning they may actually work to sabotage your company. This same research continues to show each year that a top reason that employees quit a company, or worse, "quit and stay" at a company, is a "boss from hell."

A terrible manager doesn't inspire employees and this leads to disengaged or even actively disengaged employees. This in turn can lead to a less safe work environment, waste, quality defects, poor customer service and even an increase in healthcare costs. All of these effects erode trust in the workplace. And when there is an absence of trust, it is impossible to build a healthy culture.

The Great Place to Work® Institute finds results similar to the Gallup survey. They find that trust is the core around which a triad of credibility, fairness and respect are in balance (Figure 2.3).

What is a Great Workplace?
From the Point of View of the
EMPLOYEE

A great workplace is where you trust the people you work with, have pride in what you do, and enjoy the people you work with. Any workplace can be measured through five dimensions: credibility, respect and fairness (which are attributes of trust), as well as pride and camaraderie.

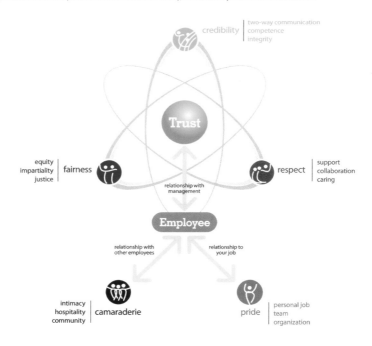

Figure 2.3 Trust Triad

Culture is defined as the shared values and beliefs of employees that are reflected in their behavior:

- How they go about doing their work
- How they interact with one another
- How they interact with customers

You have a choice with culture. You can let it evolve unintentionally and you'll get what you get. Or you can decide to make purposeful choices that will intentionally develop your culture. And, like in any new relationship, trust is one element of a healthy culture that must be nurtured and must be developed deliberately. Depending on where you are starting, it can take months if not years to develop this level of trust.

If it is left to evolve naturally, or perhaps given to HR to decide, the unintended outcome becomes a natural reflection of many individuals' tastes rather than intentional values and beliefs shared by a unified tribe. Culture is a leadership responsibility. And as Jason Fried and David Heinemeier Hansson say in *Rework*, "Culture is the by-product of consistent behavior." You've got to walk the talk.

In my experience, this cultural alignment becomes a sustainable competitive advantage that causes a company to outperform their industry and build a winning culture.

As an example, a few years ago one of our clients implemented not only our employee engagement process but also a leadership team alignment system called EOS®, or Entrepreneurial Operating System. The results were astounding. In the printing industry where margins are typically 2-3%, this company is able to achieve 8-10% margins consistently and they were having a ton of fun in the process.

Conversely, I worked with a leadership team of a small distributor several years ago. They were searching for a way to help energize the team and really felt that an employee engagement system was the right answer. I tailored the program for the company, taught the employees some basic financial acumen concepts, identified measureables, developed scorecards and mini games and an incentive plan, and set them up on a system for having their meetings. After I left though, the leadership team didn't use the scorecard. They didn't change their behavior. They didn't execute on the mini games. They didn't communicate further with the employees. Employees who were so energized and optimistic during the implementation phase began to lose hope, and they lost faith in the management team. A few of the employees contacted me independently, asking what to do. The management team had lost credibility and the culture began to crumble. They didn't do what they said they would do.

What I learned was that the company first needed alignment around a vision. The leaders needed to get on the same page, get clarity about where they were going, and then communicate that clarity to the workforce. Then the workforce would have a better chance of engaging. The owners and leadership team needed to inspire their employees, to give everyone direction and focus, and to make sure that all of the employees were 100% clear on where the company was going and how it was going to get there.

How can you expect someone to follow you if you don't know where you are going? And if you do know where you are going, but don't communicate that to your organization, you can't expect your workforce to feel connected to your vision. It's like asking people to "see what you're saying." Your vision is in your head, but your team can't see what's in your head, so you have to communicate that and get clarity and alignment on that vision.

Under the ProfitWorks LLC umbrella, we created a framework that blends leadership team alignment with employee engagement. In this way we've developed a new system that creates complete cultural alignment.

CHAPTER 3

Leadership Team Alignment - EOS® - Credibility

In *The Truth About Leadership*, James Kouzes and Barry Posner say, "If you think you're a leader and you turn around and no one is following you, then you're simply out for a walk."

A few years ago one of my clients introduced me to a leadership team alignment system called EOS®. EOS®, the Entrepreneurial Operating System®, is a holistic business system with real, simple, practical business tools that allow you to simplify, clarify and align all the pieces of your business to produce your desired results.

EOS® helps leadership teams get crystal clear about where the company is going and how they are going to get there. While reading *Traction*, by Gino Wickman, I had a light bulb moment realizing that this was the answer for so many business owners if they wanted to have success engaging their employees and building a culture of accountability, credibility, trust and profit.

As Gino developed the model, he realized that any issue an entrepreneur encounters falls into one of six business categories: Vision, People, Data, Issues, Process, and Traction (Figure 3.1).

To the degree that you can become strong, 100% strong, in each of these components, EOS® will help you do three things that we call Vision, Traction and Healthy:

- Vision: EOS® gets your leadership team 100% on the same page with the vision for your organization: who you are, what you do, where you are going and how you will get there.

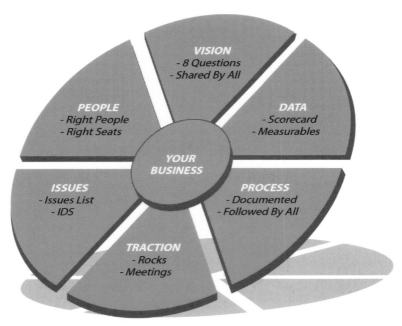

Figure 3.1 EOS® Model

- Traction: EOS® helps your leadership team become more disciplined and accountable, executing consistently to get more done and achieve every piece of your vision.
- Healthy: EOS® helps your leadership team become a healthy, functional, cohesive team, because leaders often don't function well together as a team.

From there, as goes your leadership team so goes the rest of your organization. Using this set of tools, you get to the point where your entire organization is focused and engaged and sharing a common vision. They will be disciplined, accountable, executing well and advancing as a healthy team.

Each of the six components of EOS® has two key disciplines. Within the first component, vision, the first key discipline is answering 'the eight questions' with your leadership team. The eight questions are:

1. What are your Core Values?
2. What is your Core Focus™?
3. What is your 10-Year Target™?
4. What is your Marketing Strategy?
5. What is your 3-Year Picture™?
6. What is your 1-year Plan?
7. What are your quarterly Rocks?
8. What are your Issues?

When your leadership team becomes crystal clear and 100% aligned on the answers to these questions, the culture of your company changes in an incredible way. The tool we use to help the leadership team organize the answers to these eight questions is called the Vision/Traction Organizer™ or V/TO™. Once the eight questions have been answered, it is important that this vision is shared by everyone in your company, which is the second discipline within the Vision component: Shared By All (SBA).

The second component of EOS® is People, arguably the root of most issues in any organization. The two disciplines within this component are "Right People" and "Right Seats", and as an organization, you have to have both. "Right People" means you have people in your organization who have the same core values that you discovered for your organization when we answered this under the eight questions. If you have people in your organization who do not have the same core values as you have defined, it doesn't mean they are bad people, it just means they aren't a fit for your culture. Square peg, round hole. When you remove these "misfits" from your culture, it frees you (and them), and you can pursue people who are more in line with your organization.

"Right Seats" means you have developed an Accountability Chart that clearly outlines the roles and responsibilities for each seat in your company. The Accountability Chart is an Organizational Chart on steroids. It's not just about reporting structure. It outlines your team's agreement on what the key roles are for every seat in your organization. I suggest you define the right structure for your organization before you add names. Do not build your Accountability Chart around the people you have. Focus on structure first, people second.

Once these seats have been defined, and the names have been added to the chart, you need to determine if the people in your organization have the Unique Ability®[1] to do the job as you have defined it in the roles and responsibilities for each seat. Unique Ability means they "Get the role," they "Want the role," and they have the "Capacity to do the job." And you've got to have all three.

If you have someone who shares your core values but they can't do the job, you need to make a change. And when you've got someone who can do the job, perhaps very well, but they don't share your core values, again, you have to make a change. The longer you allow either of these issues to fester, the more you anchor your company, reduce your potential for growth and remain mired in mediocrity. Within EOS®, the People Analyzer is a powerful tool you can use to help guide your decisions around this. It allows you to measure your team against your core values and also against the "Right Seats" tool. It is a very powerful, black and white tool.

The third component of EOS® is Data and the two disciplines within this component are the scorecard and the measureables. Whether you call them dashboards, scoreboards or scorecards, key performance indicators, KPIs or measureables is, of course, not important. What is important is that it is clear, simple and easy to use. I suggest five to fifteen measureables on the leadership scorecard and that you include leading indicators as well as a few of the typical lagging indicators. Each measureable should be owned by the person who has the greatest influence over the area, whether or not they have the easiest access to it. This way, if

---

[1] Unique Ability® is a registered trademark, protected by copyright and owned by The Strategic Coach® Inc. All rights reserved. Used with written permission. www.strategiccoach.com.

there is an issue related to the measureable, this "owner" can do something to solve the issue, or at least move it toward resolution.

When your team is moving toward 100% strong with the Vision component, the People component and the Data component, your organization, now much more lucid, open and honest, can more clearly identify barriers and impurities that cause friction or headaches in the daily grind. Within EOS®, these are called issues. And your company's success is directly related to your ability to solve issues.

Issues is the fourth component of EOS®. The two key disciplines are simply getting in the habit of establishing and using an Issues List in every meeting, and at every level of your organization and also using an issues processing track called IDS. IDS stands for Identify, Discuss and Solve. Most leadership teams spend their time discussing the heck out of issues, but rarely do they move to a permanent solution. Great teams acknowledge reality and avoid blame and finger-pointing. They focus on the future, move to solution quickly, and knock down a lot of issues in a short amount of time. It's an incredibly effective discipline to work through issues in an open and honest way with your team.

The fifth component is the Process component, which is probably the most overlooked aspect of business because many leaders feel it's too much minutiae or that everyone already knows the processes. After you and your team have settled on the names of the handful of core processes that exist in your business, the two key disciplines of Process are documenting those processes at a high level and then making sure everyone is following them (Followed By All). When I say at a high level, I suggest documenting the 20% of the steps that will get you 80% of the way there, which should result in a few pages (not hundreds!).

The final component of EOS® is Traction. This is where it all comes together and where the magic happens. The two key disciplines are Rocks and Meetings. Rocks are simply the 3-7 priorities (less is more) that each member of your leadership team wants to get accomplished in the next 90 days. These priorities are typically above and beyond the daily whirlwind of the roles and responsibilities of their jobs, and they are critical goals.

The second discipline, the Level-10 meeting (L10), is the weekly meeting for your leadership team where you and your leadership team use all these tools to hold each other accountable, help each other stay on track, and identify and solve any issues that may be holding you back. The L10s are an incredible discipline. After several weeks of holding these, your leadership team will feel a sense of clarity, openness and perspective on the business. And, ideally, if you are truly honest and open in these meetings, the numbers will inevitably be moving the right direction as well.

EOS® is unique because it is easy to understand and use, and it holistically addresses all issues rather than applying spot-treatments. It works in any entrepreneurial company and across all business models because the system is founded on time-tested methods and principles, not business management theories or flavor-of-the-month fads. It provides a comprehensive way of running your business, and as important, it provides a foundation of credibility upon which you can build a truly engaged workforce.

CHAPTER 4

Employee Engagement - Shared By All (SBA) - Trust

Within the EOS® model we talk about a vision that is *shared by all* (SBA) and processes that are *followed by all* (FBA). These are not trivial matters. Whether you have ten seats on your bus or 250 seats, it is critical that every one of these people shares your vision, believes your vision and is rowing in the same direction with you to achieve your vision.

The first step toward engaging everyone in the organization toward sharing your vision is to teach them a little about business. Business literacy is critical because most employees have never been taught about business and make erroneous assumptions about how much profit a company makes. These assumptions affect their behavior, and can do so in a very negative way.

Since 1996, we have asked employees, "What percent of sales is profit?" Their answers may surprise you; most employees think profit is 30-50% of sales! When your employees think your company is making this much profit, they often feel bitter and resentful because they feel they are not making enough money— someone else is—you! They think you are making all the money off their hard work, and this perpetuates division and mistrust in the culture, not to mention a lack of credibility. Additionally, if they think your company is rolling in the dough, they tend to not be tuned into waste—wasted time, wasted materials, inefficiencies, etc. Finally, this will lead your employees to believe that your company has a money tree or an unlimited source of funds and this belief often reinforces a mentality of entitlement.

Of course, what you want to create in your culture is an earning mentality. As in athletics, an earning or performance mentality exists in an organization when there is a certain amount of pressure, anxiety or stress.

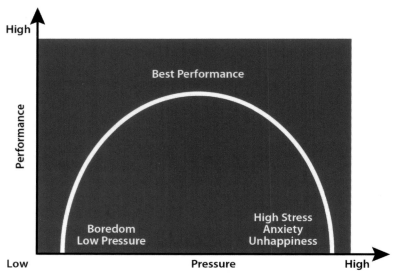

Figure 4.1 Positive Anxiety

As demonstrated in Figure 4.1, in an organization where no pressure exists and where not much is asked of employees, there are lower levels of performance. At the opposite end of the spectrum, when there is so much pressure in an organization that employees are afraid (typically top-down organizations—think 1950's style management), employees are not nearly as concerned with being productive as they are with self-preservation. They are more concerned with not getting fired or yelled at. In a culture of fear, employees are also so consumed with not failing that they tend to play it safe, and this stifles the potential for innovative ideas, risk taking and process improvements. This also leads to a lot of politics and zero-sum thinking, i.e. if you die, I live. So, there is a leadership art to creating an organization where you can have these high expectations of performance throughout the organization, and do so without creating a culture of fear.

No one wants to fail, of course. But the truth is that the potential for failure causes people to try harder to succeed. By creating the potential for failure, what we are doing in fact, is tricking ourselves into trying harder. In my experience when people have to work hard for something, there is a greater sense of accomplishment, satisfaction, and pride when they do succeed.

How people respond to failure is critical. Research shows that the mindset of the person experiencing failure is the most important indicator of how anxiety or pressure will be actively used. People who fail repeatedly tend to develop persistence in the face of challenges. They develop a habit around failure which provides them with a mindset of toughness and a resiliency toward anxiety.

Mindset becomes an important factor again when we look at employees. In *Why Employees Are Always a Bad Idea*, Chuck Blakeman differentiates between employees and stakeholders. Business coach Steve Chandler talks about the owner vs. victim mindset (Figure 4.2). In her book *Mindset*, Carol Dweck talks about the difference between a fixed mindset and a growth mindset. What all these theories have in common is the concept that a person's mindset is a choice and can therefore be taught.

Stakeholder/Owner Mentality	Victim Mentality
Independence	Dependence
I can	I should
Future-based focus	Past-based focus
Responsible	Blame and finger pointing
Delegate	Micro-management
Direction and focus	Rudderless wandering

Figure 4.2 Stakeholder vs. Victim Mentality

In my experience, this stakeholder mindset can and should be taught and reinforced because most of your employees haven't grown up with repeated exposure to basic business concepts. As a leader in your organization, it is your responsibility to teach this to your team.

Developing a stakeholder mentality throughout your workforce does a number of positive things for your company. First, when your leadership team is transparent, you send a message of respect and you build trust, which as I mentioned, is the core of culture. Business education causes your employees to look at the company like an owner does. They begin to get in the habit of seeking and sharing ways to reduce inefficiencies, and they are much more conscious of waste. When all members of a company have the eyes and ears of an owner, they begin to treat each other as partners, with a spirit of maturity and mutuality. Lastly, there is much more credibility in this new open and honest culture.

So how do you do it? How do you teach employees about business and finance, especially if you're hesitant to share detailed financials with them? Many of the books I've referenced go into more detail on how to share financials, and we've included a few key points in here to help you as well.

There's nothing magical about it, but it's important to remember that less is more. Whoever is doing the teaching needs to be dynamic and they need to have credibility. This is not an exercise left to your financial person. I actually discourage this, as they may venture into complex terminology and concepts without realizing it, and then they've lost the crowd.

Instead of looking at business literacy training as just sharing financials it is important that your employees understand what your intention is, why you are going down this path and ultimately how you as a team and they as individuals will benefit from knowing and using this information. Show them the path of where this training will take the company. They need to see the big picture of not only your intentions, but also of what's in it for them and for the entire team if they follow you down this path.

Many companies make the comparison of business to a game, where profit is the score at the end of the game. The game analogy, and keeping score, makes it less threatening than just sharing financial statements and often helps employees embrace the idea more easily.

When we teach business literacy, we use very simplified versions of financial statements to clearly illustrate the three elements of an income statement (sales minus expenses equals profit), the three elements of a cash flow statement (cash-in minus cash-out equals change in cash), and the three elements of a balance sheet (what you own equals what you owe plus what you really own). As your team becomes more familiar with these statements you can introduce more advanced concepts. Ultimately though, we want to remember the KISS rule—keep it super simple.

Your goal is to create a strong link between your employees' activities and your lagging financial statements. To the degree you can keep the conversation, the measureables and the scorecards focused on the activity-based measures that your employees really care about and can affect, you will keep the training simplified.

Remember, your goal is not to just share the financials in a one-way presentation of "how we did last quarter?" These are great opportunities for employees to begin truly owning the numbers, which is why we include a WHO column on every scorecard. You want the person with the greatest influence over the measureable to own that number and report on it. This ownership is a key tool for applying some pressure or anxiety in your culture as it causes your employees to prepare, participate and discuss their opinions and issues, not to mention to help them continue to learn and grow.

In the best companies, teaching employees about business and finance is just the way they run their organization, not just something they do once. This is why we suggest you begin the habit of communicating results with your workforce on a regular, formal basis. Many of our clients map out a formal internal communication game plan each year with specific live events, food, recognition and other engagement tools that help them reach out on a regular basis to their employees. This is a critical piece of the puzzle toward successful employee engagement. It will not be successful if you do it just once. In fact if you start down the business literacy path and then quit, you will actually do more damage to your credibility than if you hadn't done anything. You will be perceived as having just undertaken another flavor-of-the-month initiative.

As your team gets more comfortable with driving the measureables on a regular basis, undoubtedly you will encounter a measureable from time to time that is consistently out of whack. A great tool to get everyone focused on improving that number is to set up a fun challenge (in *The Great Game of Business*, Jack Stack calls them MiniGames™; in *Ownership Thinking*™, Brad Hams calls them Rapid Improvement Plans). These games can be companywide, or often they may be departmental or by business unit. When you design a game, it's important not to overthink it. Simply set up a challenge to move the number from X to Y in 90 days. The path to what winning looks like must be very clear. And when the team wins a game, celebrate!

Games are a great tool because they blend a financial focus with a culture of participation. It's that healthy and smart thing again. Soft and hard. Yin and Yang. Balance. They're fun, and they're also designed to drive improvements in the business that will help the employees actively participate and win in two ways. First, they win through the celebration at the end of a game. Secondly, they help fund a profit-sharing plan, which I'll talk briefly about below.

I must caution you with the games: even though they are fun and add an element of camaraderie and accomplishment to the culture, don't feel the need to wrap a game around every measureable you have. If fun is not part of your culture, don't force it. There's nothing more awkward than telling your employees that they have to have fun. It must happen more naturally than that. If games and challenges aren't your thing, consider prioritizing the improvement goal as someone's quarterly "rock."

As you begin to engage your employees by teaching business literacy, and providing tools like measureables, scorecards, Level 10 meetings, and mini games, it is also critical to design and implement a simple profit-sharing plan, creating a win-win situation. Although we find that most employees are not only motivated by money, a profit-sharing plan sends a message of shared goals, reward and team performance. In *Why Employees Are Always a Bad Idea*, Chuck Blakeman says that because stakeholders participate in profit creation, through changed behavior and profit improvement efforts, they should also participate in profit-sharing. In my experience, although this is not a deal breaker, it does help you establish credibility for your initiative, and it draws the attention of any fence-sitters in your organization. If we can get the 50% of your employees whom Gallup says are disengaged to begin to engage because there is a profit-sharing plan, then I'd score that as a win.

Many profit-sharing plans become entitlements because there is such a weak link between the activities of the employees and the financial results in your company. In order for this not to occur, your profit-sharing plan needs to not only be simple, but it also has to be discussed frequently, at least quarterly, within your internal communications game plan. It can't be just a once-a-year message. Done right, a simple cash-based profit-sharing plan is a great opportunity for leaders to reconnect the dots for everyone, and reinforce that everyone should always be looking to reduce inefficiencies and waste, as well as recognize and seize new opportunities for growth.

Lastly, it can happen that too much focus on the financial payout of a profit-sharing plan diminishes its attraction for employees.

It may be perceived as a hollow carrot for your employees. We use the term healthy and smart to help bolster this. As we've discussed, healthy and smart are the yin-yang of business and you've got to have both. The smart side of the profit-sharing plan is the financial payout. Employees certainly love the payout. In my 19 years of doing this, I've only seen one occasion where an employee didn't want the payout, and that person soon after decided that they weren't a fit in the organization. But I've found there is a fine line between celebrating by providing a financial reward for the team and making it the only reason you are engaging with the employees. As a leader, it is important that your motives are pure when it comes to the incentive, and this purity needs to be expressed frequently so your employees know your aim is true. It goes back to trust and credibility.

In addition to financial rewards, many companies include non-financial rewards to recognize employees, have some fun and create some healthy internal competition. There are multiple books on this topic. If you're interested, I'd encourage you to read Bob Nelson's *1001 Ways to Reward Employees*. Rest assured, done with an honest heart, these efforts will absolutely help support your efforts to engage the workforce.

CHAPTER 5

Moving Forward

EOS® and these SBA (Shared By All) employee engagement tools are proven methodologies that not only improve the financial performance of your firm, but also create a winning culture of trust in your firm. Leaders who commit to the principles outlined in this short book can transform their companies in a very short time. When there is clarity among your leadership team, that clarity leads to credibility and trust within your culture. And when you have a culture built on that firm foundation of trust, you have a path toward the engagement of everyone in the organization. It's truly incredible what your team can do when everyone knows where to look and is rowing in the same direction.

By getting the leadership team to speak the same language, to walk the talk, and to hold each other accountable on a regular, formal basis, your numbers will start moving in the right direction. I guarantee it.

AFTERWORD

My business partner and I successfully conquered Mt. Kilimanjaro on Sept. 29, 2014. The "high" that we experienced was truly even higher than the summit itself.

Our trek was a predetermined reward for accomplishing our business goals. We had formalized our business arrangement less than one year before. We are well-versed in the best practices of the Entrepreneurial Operating System® (EOS®) as well as employee engagement and Ownership Thinking™. By "practicing what we preach," so to speak, we exceeded our goals well beyond our expectations. We took this trip not only in celebration, but also as our "Clarity Trip™" retreat to plan the short-, mid-, and long-term strategies that would support our future financial success and fulfill our personal mission to help other entrepreneurs.

Even on the mountain, the principles of EOS® came in to play. Halfway up our climb, our guide left us. To be fair, his wife was having an emergency appendectomy. But it did cause us more than a little concern; we had 6,000 vertical feet to go (the peak is at 19,341 feet). The assistant guide spoke very poor English; everyone else spoke none! How would we communicate in an emergency? How would we get to the top? Who would manage the porters?

We shouldn't have worried. These guides understand that "stuff happens," and that safety is paramount to their livelihoods. Each adjusted to their newly assumed role in the Accountability Chart with ease. An Accountability Chart and Succession Planning in Tanzania? It was clear they had planned for and discussed situations like this. The Assistant Guide became the Lead Guide; the Head Porter became the Assistant Guide. Everyone just carried a little more weight – literally. Even with the language barrier, we clearly understood the new hierarchy and were immeasurably impressed by the transition. It made us ask ourselves, "How many businesses are braced for an unexpected change in leadership, or for a change in the business landscape due to external forces beyond their control?"

We returned renewed, and with clarity of vision and a commitment to new goals. We've set new travel adventures in our sights, and these motivate us every day to stay focused and better support our clients.

This is what this book was all about when I wrote it—to document how to create a vision and achieve it—for yourself and for your company. I'm happy to say I've not only seen it work, but I've tested it and proven that it works. I wish you success on your journey.

ACKNOWLEDGEMENTS

Thanks to Dad for introducing me to the importance of business acumen at all levels of an organization. Thanks to Mom, for encouraging me, teaching me discipline, and always emphasizing the positive. Thanks to Tom Bouwer, for your limitless energy and your willingness to pursue this passion with me, and thanks also to my brothers and to the ProfitWorks LLC team for your encouragement. Lastly, my heartfelt thanks to the late Brad Hams, founder of Ownership Thinking™, for inspiring and mentoring me.

This eBook isn't finished. I invite your questions, suggestions and comments and will work to incorporate them into future editions. You may repurpose this material on your blog, in a newsletter, or whatever platform you feel best reaches those who will benefit from reading it. Kindly provide attribution when doing so. You can't edit it, sell it or offer it conjunction with something that's sold. I hope this inspires you to write your own eBook and to also find and interact with ProfitWorks LLC on our social media platforms. I look forward to continuing the dialogue.

ABOUT THE AUTHOR AND PROFITWORKS

Alex Freytag has holistic career-experience that guides his passion to help entrepreneurs achieve higher levels of employee engagement and greater business success. He is a Certified EOS® Implementer and Partner at ProfitWorks LLC, which he co-founded in 1996. He is a lifelong entrepreneur and has consulted with hundreds of companies, helping them experience new levels of growth and cultural health.

Alex has extensive experience in all functional areas of business. He was responsible for developing new product offerings at Elmer's Products and revitalizing and refocusing business operations at a century-old chocolate manufacturer. He most recently led the leadership team at Ownership Thinking, a company dedicated to creating cultures of employees who think and act like owners. With his confident and insightful approach, he is passionate about helping companies gain traction and greater performance.

A sought-after public speaker, Alex delivers high-value content by sequentially building on concepts and engaging his audiences in a robust Q &A. His presentation style ensures that attendees leave with practical new skills and knowledge relevant to their business issues. A top-ranked Vistage speaker, he presents internationally to the CEO and C-level members of this world-class executive organization.

Alex is an active member of the ESOP Association and a current Advisory Board member for the NCEO, attending their regional and national conferences throughout the year. He earned his B.A. in Psychology from Hamilton College, his MBA from The

Max. M. Fisher College of Business at The Ohio State University and was class Valedictorian for his graduate program.

Alex and his wife, Christine, live in Columbus, Ohio with their three children, Alec, Sophia and Ethan.

If you're interested in implementing EOS® and bringing these Shared By All (SBA) employee engagement tools into your company, please contact Alex through his company's website at www.profitworksllc.com.

Profit*Works*

INDEX

Clarity Trip™ is a trademark of ProfitWorks LLC.

The following are trademarks and integral concepts owned by EOS® Worldwide. All rights reserved. Used with written permission. www.eosworldwide.com.

- 10-Year Target™
- 3-Year Picture™
- Clarity Break™
- Core Focus™
- Entrepreneurial Operating System®
- EOS®
- The Vision/Traction Organizer™
- Traction®